AWN
2000

D0057201

A Lion's Hunger

POEMS OF FIRST LOVE

By Ann Turner
Illustrations by Maria Jimenez

Marshall Cavendish New York

Marshall Cavendish,
99 White Plains Road,
Tarrytown, New York 10591

Library of Congress Cataloging-in-Publication Data
Turner, Ann Warren.
A lion's hunger / Ann Turner.
p. cm.
Summary: Poems follow a year in a girl's life as she meets a boy, starts dating him, falls in love, and sees their special relationship come to an end.
ISBN 0-7614-5035-1
1. Dating (Social customs)—Juvenile poetry. 2. Children's poetry, American. 3. Love poetry, American. [1. Dating (Social customs)—Poetry. 2. Love—Poetry. 3. American poetry.] I. Title.
PS3570.U665L56 1999 811'.54—dc21 98-10865 CIP AC

The text of the book is set in 12 point Cochin.
The illustrations are oil on stretched canvas.
Printed in the United States of America
First edition

6 5 4 3 2 1

September 12

A new boy today,
lanky for a change,
instead of short and squat
who talks only of cars.
This one has long, lean legs,
a quick smile,
and where he sat
there was laughter,
like ripples around a stone.
I am definitely interested.

October 1

He can talk!

We walked together,

he spoke of books

(books!), travel, a trip

out West (drinking and horses).

People think that sex is about bodies—

it isn't.

It's about talk, about words

curling up out of the lips like smoke

so sweet it pulls me in—

I wonder where we're going.

October 10

I think he exists

for me,

that he was put here

to fill the emptiness

that is me.

I eat his words, his smile

the way his hands move

through air.

I am dancing

inside.

November 1

The air smells different,
  sharper, cleaner,
    the ground springs up
      under my feet;
food tastes like colors,
  purple, orange, flaming red—
    I guess this
      is love.

November 10

The history of our first date
is inscribed in my mind:
how you forgot the movie's name,
how I left my scarf draped
over the still-warm seat,
how we almost missed
our ride home.
I know this is the beginning
of love—this map
to the country
where only we two walk.

November 25

Thanksgiving time —

a dead bird, turnips, potatoes,

mounds of food I cannot eat.

I am tasting your mouth —

not food.

I am drinking your eyes —

not wine.

I am filling myself

with you

and I cannot eat.

December 2

The sweater smells

of you,

where you held me—

a sharp, lime scent—

the stripes are imbued with you.

I hide it under my pillow

so no one can ask why

I won't wash it.

It will stay there

forever.

December 10

Your hand reaches

out

mine stretches to meet,

the space ignites—

flame

on

flame.

January 3

When you are gone

there is a gnawing ache

inside

a toothless space,

a lion's hunger

to be fed.

January 14

Mother cleaned my room,
  holding out my sweater
    like a dusty rag.
What, she asked,
  what, what, why?
The words pelted
  over my shoulders,
    I shrugged,
      pretended
        I'd forgotten.
Did she ever know?
  Did she never press her nose
    into cloth,
      inhaling love?

February 1

No one knows
what I am doing
standing here
where you stood
yesterday.
My feet are taking you in,
sucking you up
so that I can last
until I see you
again.

February 8

I am getting you
by heart,
learning the gull's wing
of your eyebrow,
the curve where your ear
meets your neck,
the sudden way you pause
for breath.

February 25

You didn't come!
I waited by the bank
under the sign
that slowly twirled round,
looking for your green coat,
looking for your loping walk.
But all I saw were two dogs,
an old lady in pink curlers,
and a man yelling into a phone.
What happened? So soon
are we unraveling?

March 1

I will always love
white jeans.
When you came
to pick me up,
you leaned against
the rail,
your legs so long and lean,
encased
in white
they seemed
a talisman.

March 8

I love how your body
is different from mine—
  where I go out, you
    go in;
where I am soft,
  you are firm;
where you knife the sky,
  I am close to the earth.

So different, but the way we fit
  is ordained.

March 20

I am making a religion
of love —
rituals, perfume,
hands clasped always
yours over mine (right over left);
a kiss before we talk,
a late night phone call —
one ring only
to tell me you're thinking of me.
I am dedicated,
I am sincere,
I am its priestess.

April 3

We walked through the woods,
wind scouring our faces,
taking your words away.
I reached for them,
suddenly afraid,
and the sun faltered
on the path ahead.
Blackness opened inside
when I thought of a path
without you,
of air without your smell,
without your words,
your salt skin.

April 5

We studied Walt Whitman today,
Out of the Cradle Endlessly Rocking.
The words took me, as if
I were in your arms and we
had flown to some far space
where the stars bent down
to say hello...
When the bell rang I woke,
shocked and drowning
in the present.

April 7

I gave you the book,

we shared a poem

and some sticky crumbs from lunch—

all I can expect to be fed

this day.

April 15

They tell us

we are lucky—

that we were not killed,

that the other couple

is safe.

Stupid, stupid, we drank

red wine,

drove in the blinding rain,

and skidded that terrible,

long, black way into

the other car.

You are stitched—I am also,

and we are forbidden

to see each other.

That is not lucky.

May 1

Your voice is thin

over the phone, all

we are allowed.

I cup my hand,

as if I could catch you

in my palm

and drink you down.

May 5

Reprieve, I don't know how.

They guessed that we would meet,

no matter what.

Now we can walk together,

talk—not drive—

but at least I am not

famished

for the sight of you.

May 12

Somehow that accident
smashed something inside,
hurt something I did not know
could be hurt.
You are distant,
don't phone,
my stitches are out,
but I don't see how
I can heal.

May 24

Reckless promises. You

said things, bargained,

sealed our future with words—

empty and hollow

as an echoing drainpipe.

My chest hurts, as if you

had slammed a fist

into it.

May 30

I am remembering
 the feel of you,
  the nub of your hands,
the way your smile crooked
 up, and how your legs stretched
  the length of me.
I have you by heart,
 and that is all
  I have.

June 2

I am throwing stones
into the river where we walked;
each stone a promise unmet,
a glance gone wrong,
a word lost in space.
Stones plummet and dive
through the water
to the muddy bottom
of my heart.

June 3

It is the sudden memories

I cannot stand—

how the rain falling

on a night street

reminds me—

how the smoke from a bus

jerks me back—

how a crooked smile

on someone else's face

makes me cry.

It will take a long time

to dig you

out of my heart.

June 5

If I just do everything
differently,
I will be all right.
Get out of bed
on the left side.
Wash my face *before*
brushing my teeth.
Change my perfume,
cut my hair.
And then I will be rid
of your smell,
the stamp you put
on me.

June 8

My parents think
I'm crazed, that somehow
ours was just a beginner love,
like someone learning to drive.
Is love only for grownups?
Do you have to graduate
first?
They will never know
the lion's hunger
inside of me.

June 11

You waved today,
pretending, I see,
that we could be
friends.
I turned and walked away.
Never, never, never!
You are cast off, cast out,
nada.

June 12

Do the same stars
  that look down on me
    look down on you?
Does their clean light
  settle on your shoulders
    too?
Why don't the moon and stars
  seal up their light
    for those who lie?

June 14

Enough. I am tired
of mourning you.
Today I buried your photograph
by the tree
where we first kissed.
The bracelet—dug into the soil.
The ring—covered up.
I will write a new history,
without you.
I will fall in love
with myself.

July 6

I did it!

I went out

with someone else.

Not in white jeans, not

smelling like you,

not with the same

crazy jokes.

But I survived. Almost,

I enjoyed myself.

For one sweet moment,

I forgot.

July 15

I saw today
that the sun shone.
A bird called outside,
and suddenly,
I was hungry again.
Not with that black, aching
emptiness,
but just tooth-hungry,
mouth-hungry
for food and milk and
sweet things.

July 30

Oh, lion's hunger,

was it worth it?

So much joy

between us;

such words I have never known,

the sinking down into you—empty—

and coming up—full.

Someday I will know

what we had.

When lines crease my face,

and children tug

at my shirt,

I will know.

But that is

a lifetime away.

August

Someday will someone
dig up the root
of that old tree
and find
a tattered photograph, a ring,
a corroded bracelet,
and wonder why they're there?
Maybe all that passion left
a mark on those old things
and when their fingers touch
your image,
they will burn.